Cool Open String Licks
A BEGINNER'S GUIDE

By Kyle Carmean

Recording Credits:
Toby Wine, Guitar

Cover artwork by Levin Pfeufer

Cherry Lane Music Company
Educational Director/Project Supervisor: Susan Poliniak
Director of Publications: Mark Phillips
Publications Coordinator: Rebecca Skidmore

ISBN 978-1-57560-921-8

Copyright © 2010 Cherry Lane Music Company
International Copyright Secured   All Rights Reserved

The music, text, design and graphics in this publication are protected by copyright law. Any duplication or transmission,
by any means, electronic, mechanical, photocopying, recording or otherwise, is an infringement of copyright.

Visit our website at www.cherrylaneprint.com

Contents

Introduction

Every instrument has its own unique characteristics that, when understood, can further your musical expression. One of the main features of the guitar is its open strings. With the exception of playing an open string, every note must be played with two hands—one hand to fret the note and the other to pluck or "attack" the string. Having freedom of movement in your frethand can open up a world of possibilities when playing chords and solo lines. Using an open string with chords can allow an otherwise unreachable extra note to sustain into the next chord. This technique can also add color and speed to your improvising and give you that extra moment to set up your next phrase. All of the guitar greats handle the open strings in their own way. Angus Young, Jimmy Page, Steve Vai, Pat Metheny, Keller Williams, and Allan Holdsworth are just a small handful of artists who have their own unique approach to using the open strings in their soloing and songwriting. Even if some of the genres of music explored in this book are unfamiliar to you, take some time and check them out. Every style has something to offer whether it be in chord colors, form, solo ideas, or song writing. If any examples give you trouble, take the tempo down a couple of notches and work it out. Slowly increase the speed until it is comfortable to play at the given tempo. You can even practice the examples faster than indicated. Eventually, you'll be able to develop your own approach to using open strings.

I hope you enjoy playing through these licks as much as I enjoyed writing them!

Note: Track 1 contains tuning pitches.

About the Author

Kyle has toured the country and recently performed in an Off-Broadway rendition of the musical *Man of La Mancha*. He has worked with a variety of musicians, including John Robinson of the Quincy Jones Orchestra, Jeff Tamelier and Barry Danielian from Tower of Power, Bill Watrous, Gil Parris, John Abercrombie, Charles Blenzig, Jim Rotondi, Randy Johnston, Jose Madero from the Tito Puente Orchestra, and Rich Morales of Spyro Gyra. Kyle is featured as the composer, arranger, and producer on his newly completed debut album. He currently teaches music theory, guitar master classes, and ensembles; writes arrangements; and performs extensively for Lagond Music in Elmsford, New York, where he has been employed since 2003. Kyle also teaches privately in the Greenwich, Connecticut and Westchester, New York areas.

Acknowledgments

This book is dedicated to Karen and Robert Carmean for always encouraging and supporting me, to Susan and John for the opportunities and experience, and to Jacqui for being there when I need her.

Rock

In the first measure of the first rock lick below, the E before the bend should be played with a downstroke. This will allow you to continue with another downstroke into the following G-string bend. You will need to play both bends with your ring finger because the strings are harder to bend that far down on the neck.

TRACK 02

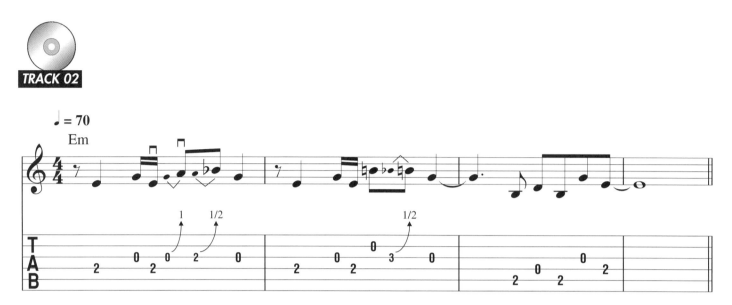

This next riff is exclusively *double stops* (two notes played at the same time), and every double stop is based on the 6th interval. Always use two fingers for fretting phrases like this—you want to have independent control of each note at all times. I prefer to use the middle and ring fingers for riffs with 6ths in them. This method also applies to parallel fingerings. If you just barre your finger across the strings for parallel fingerings, you will lose speed and flexiblity, and have problems if one of the notes needs to change suddenly. In beat 3 of the first measure, the B could be played on the open string, but parallel fingering is more useful here, especially at a fast tempo.

If you are using two fingers to play this riff, you can choose either to pick right across the strings in a raking motion or utilize a "hybrid" style by simultaneously picking the lower note and plucking the higher note at the same time. If you decide to pick across the strings, you should mute the middle string with your middle finger.

TRACK 03

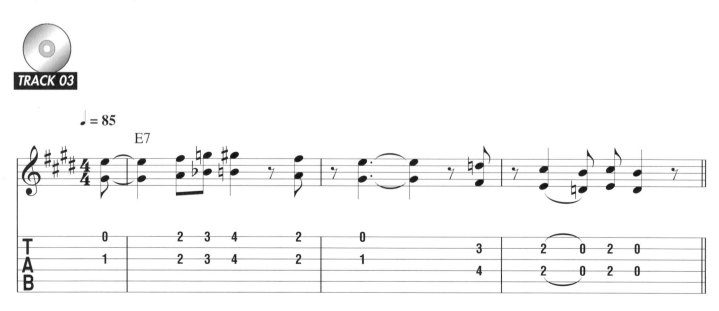

Here we have a solo line over a very common chord progression that resembles the one from "Sweet Home Alabama." This is at a slow tempo, so don't let the 16th note run scare you. The open B and E strings help to spell out a D major pentatonic scale. The phrase shifts slightly to compensate for the C chord in the next measure. To get a feel for the first 16th note rest, really hear and feel the downbeat of the first measure, and then start the phrase immediately after the downbeat—this is how I think of that 16th note rest in the beginning of the lick. In the second measure, *alternate picking* (picking in alternating downstrokes and upstrokes, often beginning with a downstroke on the first downbeat) becomes crucial to bending the A on the G string. In this case, you'll want to attack that A with a strong upstroke. Silently release the bend before hitting the beat 3 pull-off, and you're almost home sweet home.

TRACK 04

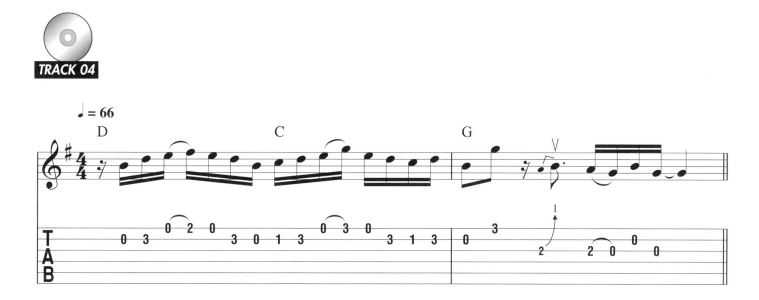

This next example uses a technique I enjoy: You play one of the lower strings as a *pedal tone* (a kind of repeated "anchoring" note) while playing a double stop or single-note motif above it. The double stops on the strings adjacent to the open A pedal tone allow you to dig in while strumming. Be sure to mute the dead notes (indicated by an "x") in the first measure. If you play this with a hybrid picking style, you probably won't be able to get the "chunky" sound that the traditional picking style will give you. The pull-off in the last measure will give you time to set up the following string skip.

TRACK 05

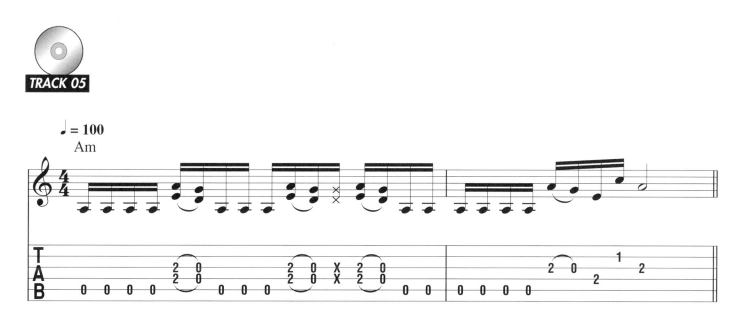

Here's how you can use the open strings during the introduction of a song. This riff sets up the key of A major by means of an E7 chord. Play the three fretted notes on the B string with your pinky, middle, and index fingers, respectively. Make sure that the open high E-string notes ring out for their full durations. This is important in slow rock licks like this one. Pay attention to your tone, and make sure that your upstrokes are nice and clear.

TRACK 06

Next up is another intro riff, only this time it's in the key of G major. The G on beat 4 will give your pick-hand enough time to set up that big, open G chord that begins the song.

TRACK 07

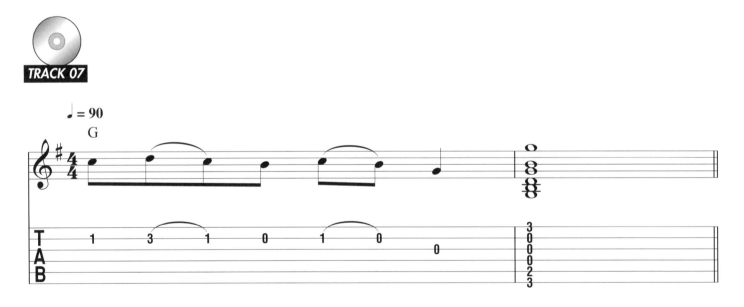

On the top of the next page is the same riff from the first measure above again, just compressed and played twice as fast. Notice the addition of rests on beats 1 and 2 of the first measure.

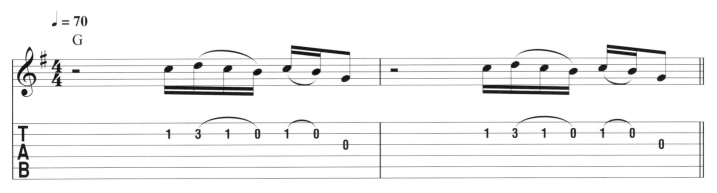

This next example is an open-string lick à la Eric Clapton; the riff and chord progression remind me of the tune "Wonderful Tonight." Set the pickup selector to the bridge, dial up some crunch on the amp, and have at it.

Sliding is an effective way to change position while still setting up a "base" for you to land. Play the slide in the first measure with your middle finger—you'll be in position for the D and ready to slide right back down to open position. In the second measure, you'll need to concentrate on getting the downstroke of beat 2 tight. Notice how the open strings and slides function with the G and D chords in the first and second measures, as opposed to those chords in the fourth and fifth measures. A musical phrase that stays more or less the same over different chords can create a very memorable and lyrical feel. When you are soloing, it is important to think melodically, and this is especially true on guitar. It's important to understand that many instruments are powered by breath. When I'm soloing, I always try to phrase my lines with my breathing. Try it for yourself. Take a breath, solo as you breathe out, and stop playing when you run out of breath. As you get used to this and begin to breathe more naturally, you should notice that your phrases start to cross over the beat and barline easily. This allows you to play more freely and naturally—more like a horn player or a singer.

TRACK 09

Make sure to play this next lick cleanly. Don't let the the open E in first measure bleed into the next measure. Experiment with the bend in measure 3. Try bending it in both directions—up and then down—to see which way is the most comfortable for you. The benefit here is that the middle strings allow plenty of room to make bends in both directions.

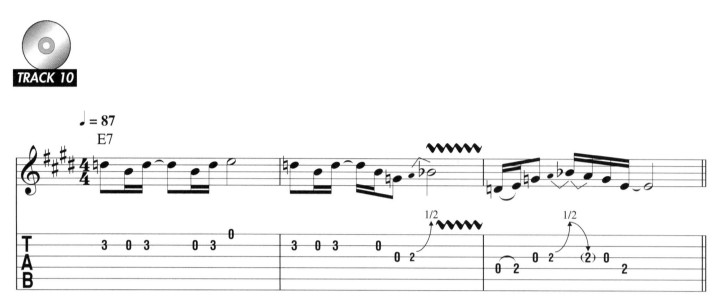

Keep one or two fingers grouped behind your bending finger for strength. You'll need the extra bending power the closer you get to the nut. When executing the vibrato in the first measure, make sure that the open G string doesn't ring out as you move to the notes on the D string.

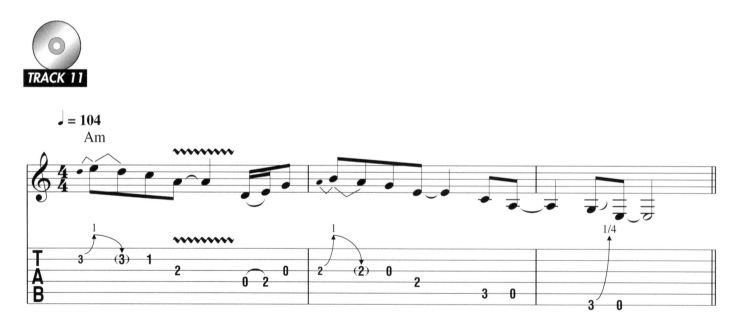

Try all downstrokes as well as alternate picking for the open strings in this example. I think you'll find that a little gain or distortion on your amp will make the open strings sound gritty and better suit the style.

Be prepared to use your pinky to play the E♭ at the end of the first measure. You'll have to hold the C bend on beat 4 with your ring finger while you play the E♭ with your pinky. Also, remember to keep your index and middle fingers behind your ring finger for bending strength.

This riff will help develop your accuracy at bending half and whole steps. In the first measure, play the upbeats as upstrokes and really choke the end of the first bend. You will need to choke the bend in the second measure as well, but do so with your freting hand. Make sure you attack the open G string cleanly after the bend. Also, use your middle finger at the beginning of the second measure, and then switch to your index finger for the E in beat 2—this will make the trill easier to play.

TRACK 14

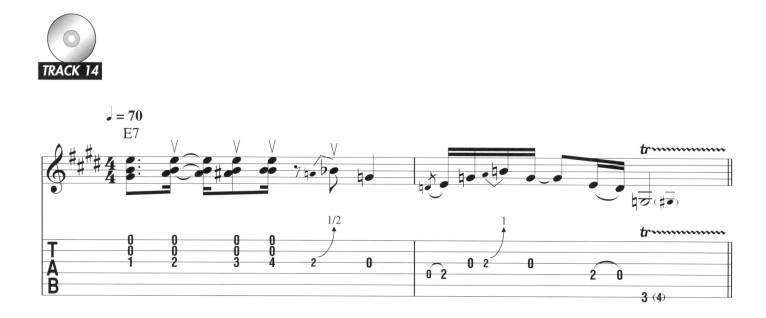

Blues

In the next example, you will have to play in a hybrid picking style, incorporating both pick and fingers. Try playing the double stops first by picking, and then using the hybrid style. The hybrid style is more applicable here because it gives you greater control over the way a phrase is articulated, regardless of how many strings are between the two notes that are to be played. Play the lower note with the pick and the top note with your middle finger. The motif will work, with minimal adjustment, over every chord in an E blues. This example is a medium shuffle using the E minor pentatonic scale (E–G–A–B–D) with a few embellished notes. Notice how the top note of each phrase incorporates the use of an open string. Pay some consideration to the hammer-ons in this example; these articulations help give the line a more rhythmic feel. Having the two triplet phrases played as hammer-ons will keep your pickhand on track, especially at faster tempos.

TRACK 15

Here is the same riff as before, except over an A7 chord with a loose Charleston rhythm in the last measure. For those of you who weren't alive during the 1920s, this is a dotted quarter note–based rhythm that started a dance craze. Be sure to fret the strings with your fingertips, as otherwise those open strings will be muffled.

TRACK 16

Next up is a lick used over the *turnaround* section of a 12-bar blues. A turnaround is generally the last two or four bars of a blues chorus—it gets you back to the beginning of the 12-bar progression. This particular turnaround is played over measures 9–12 of a 12-bar blues chorus. Rhythmically, this melodic line is similar to the previous two examples, except that the triplet in the first measure has been converted to a quarter note. Whatever picking approach you used in the previous examples should work here as well. In the second measure, after the double stop with the slide, play the phrase on beats 3–4 with your middle finger barred across both strings. If you have trouble with the double pull-offs in the second measure, try using your middle finger on the G string and your ring finger on the B string. That fingering should comfortably resemble a traditional open A chord, making it easier to perform the pull-offs. Remember, when there are strings between the double stops, or when the double stops aren't on the same fret, playing them with different fingers is recommended. Notice that the last double stop in the lick anticipates the E7 chord. When you feel as if you are running out of steam, anticipations like this can help to propel the tune forward.

TRACK 17

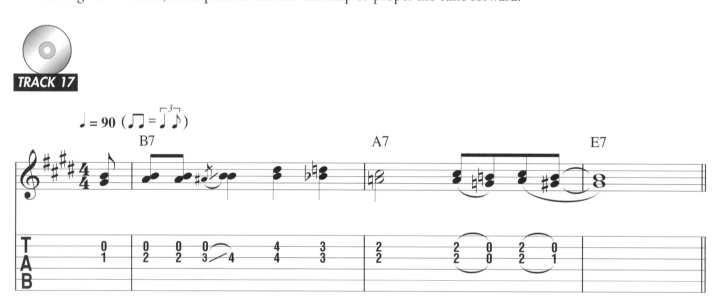

This lick has a Steve Miller Band vibe to it. The two consecutive open strings in the first measure require you to perform a mute with your frethand so that the notes last only for their specified values. In the second measure, the bend needs to be silenced quickly. Make sure your bend is nice and staccato—you don't want it bleeding into your next note.

TRACK 18

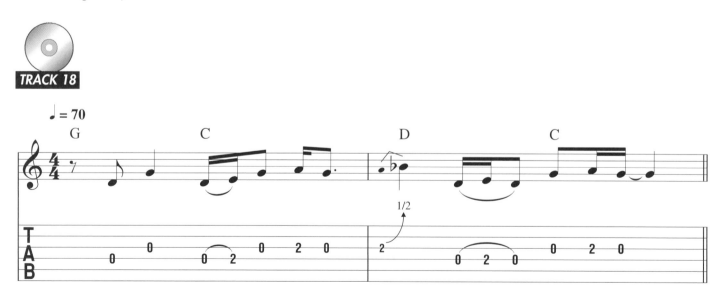

The lick on the top of the next page is a descending line underneath the open E string. The upbeats are accented to give propulsion to the line. Get up on those frethand fingertips! That open E string needs to come through loud and clear.

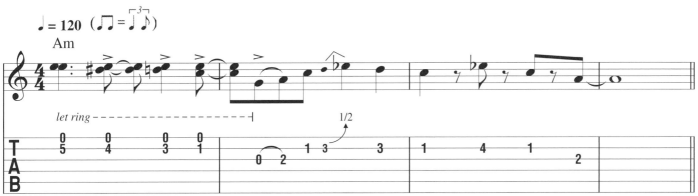

Don't barre the double stops here—use either your index and middle fingers, or your middle and ring fingers—and this slide with your ring finger will be a piece of cake. When you get to the bend in the second measure, keep some fingers behind for support.

Notice how the B on the middle line of the treble clef can be executed differently. You can play it on the G string for slides and bends, or on the open B string itself for its sustain. In the first measure, play the F and F♯ with your middle and ring fingers, respectively. This will allow you to play the A comfortably with your index finger.

In this example, don't let the open strings ring longer than their stated values, as doing otherwise would muddle the phrasing. At the two consecutive bends, be sure to release the first bend silently by muting the strings with your bending finger.

TRACK 22

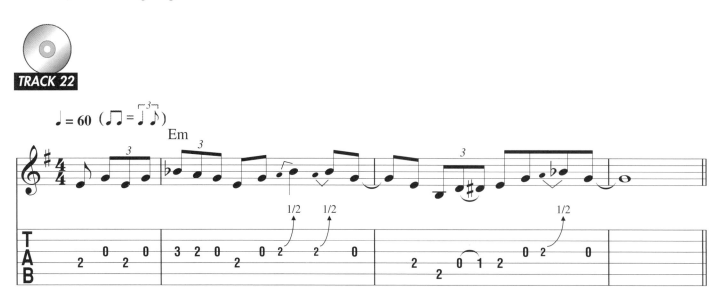

Keep your frethand in open position so that your fingers are lined up for both bends with your ring finger. On those lower-string bends, pull each bend "toward the floor," as otherwise you'll run out of fretboard.

TRACK 23

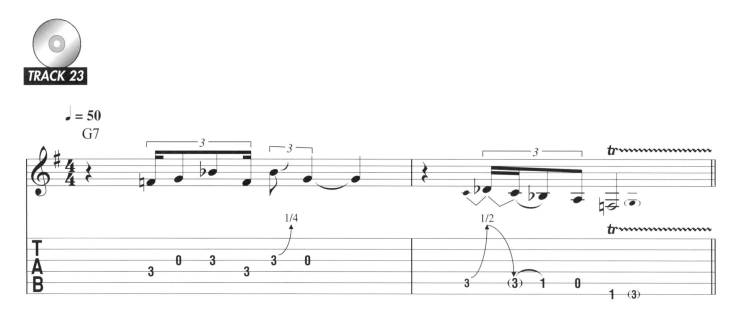

On this next lick, be sure to play all of the upbeats with strong upstrokes, especially those marked with the staccato (short) accent in the first measure. Keep your fingers lined up on the frets so you can quickly release the bend to the following note.

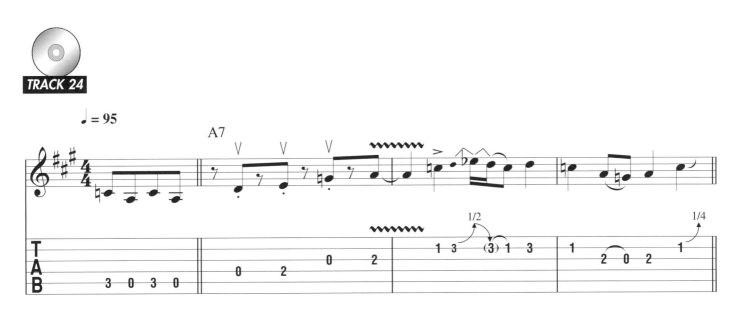

This riff starts in E major pentatonic (E–F♯–G♯–B–C♯) and then finishes in E minor pentatonic (E–G–A–B–D). In the first measure, when you move from the G-string hammer-on to the B string, don't let the G string ring sympathetically—use your pickhand to mute it to ensure a clean transition.

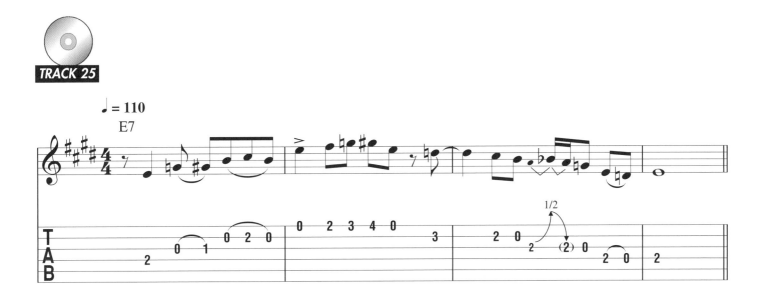

Country

Depending on the size of your hand, playing on the E, B, and G strings is best accomplished when your fret-hand thumb is positioned parallel with the neck. If your hand is larger than average, some of the stretch needed to play on these strings can be accomplished by having your thumb a little more perpendicular to the neck.

This next riff contains a *hemiola*. A hemiola is a phrase that has a rhythmic ratio of 3:2. In other words, in the course of three beats, a phrase will repeat itself twice instead of three times. Look for the hemiola in beats 1–3 of the first measure; the eighth note phrase C–C♯–E repeats twice in beats 1–3. If you follow those notes into measure 2, the hemiola will finally end in beat 2—that's a total of six beats containing four repetitions, again a ratio of 3:2. This example shows us how hammer-ons can ease the complicated picking of hemiolas and other odd-numbered note groupings. Playing the hemiola requires a slight adjustment to the usual picking situation. You should still use alternate picking, but here you need to play a downstroke on the beginning of every hammer-on and an upstroke on the open E string. This phrase repeats four times, so if you pick as described, you'll be prepared with a downstroke for beat 3 in the second measure.

TRACK 26

In the first measure, the quarter note on beat 2 will give you enough time to wind up for a strong attack of the double stop on beat 3. The rest of the phrase is based on the upbeats. Be sure to play each upbeat note with an upstroke—doing so will prepare your picking for a downstroke on beat 3 of the third measure. If you have trouble with the open E and B strings ringing out between hammer-ons, adjust your thumb on the back of the neck and make sure to play with your fingertips.

TRACK 27

Even in this style of music, a *drone note* (the same note held or played repeatedly, as seen in measure 1) is an effective melodic device. This phrase is based on groupings of five eighth notes. Odd-numbered groupings like this create a sort of "built-in" alternating picking accent for the phrase. Play the first double stop with a downstroke, use an upstroke for the next, and then play a downstroke once again for the last double stop in measure 2. In measure 3, use your middle finger for the slide and then your index finger for the D on the B string. For the second slide, be sure to stick to the alternate picking.

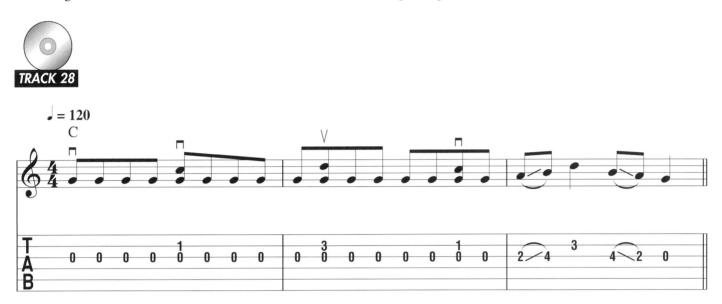

Here's another fast groove with double stops. Try playing this line with all downstrokes, as this will add uniformity to the sound of the phrase. If it's not obvious, use your index and middle fingers to fret the notes. Dynamics are a very important aspect of musical phrasing. Pay close attention to your dynamics and really concentrate on using your frethand to mute or sustain the notes accordingly. Being aware of dynamics will give you a jump-start on frethand control.

At the top of the next page we have a D major pentatonic riff that starts on the 6th (B). Combining the hammer-on and pull-off in beats 1–2 makes playing this quick rhythmic phrase much easier. Make sure that your bends stay "in time," rhythmically. This is very important to the phrasing of the lick. In the second measure, you will also want to wind up for the attack of the 16th note in beat 2. This will help propel the riff through the trill in beats 3–4.

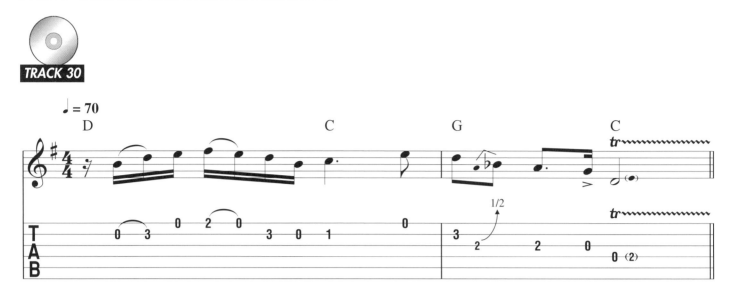

TRACK 30

This example has a nice rolling tempo and a classic country guitar feel. Play the first note short and force yourself to continue to alternate your pick strokes throughout the phrase. As for the previous examples, consistently using alternate picking here will prepare you for the strong downbeat needed in beat 4.

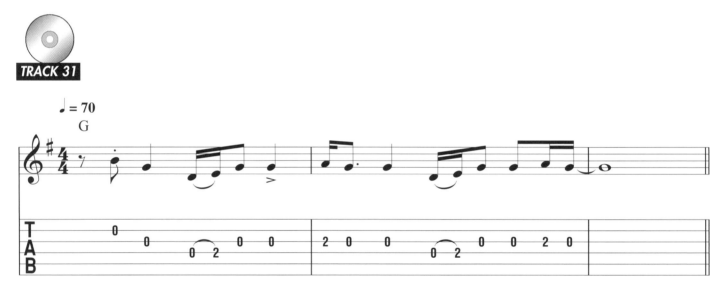

TRACK 31

The key to getting this example is in nailing the double hammer-on. Stylistically, this adds to the true flavor of the lick. The melodic content is a combination of notes similar to both the C and G major pentatonic scales. You could argue that a slide might be more appropriate for the triplets, but that far down on the neck, there isn't enough room to set yourself up for a slide.

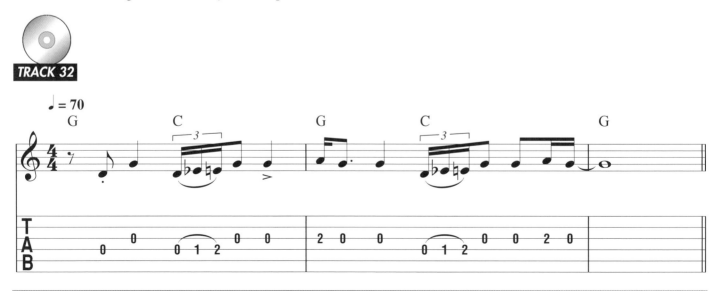

TRACK 32

Use your middle finger for the slides in this lick. At 80 b.p.m., the quarter note can get lengthy, so really take your time through the bend in beat 4 and remember to use both your index and middle fingers behind the bend for support. At the end of measure 2, be sure to play that quick little slide with an upstroke. In measures 3–4, notice that the phrase can be manipulated over the Em chord as well. In the third measure, make sure to accent the last E for the slide in beat 4.

This example uses the same drone idea as before. Here, it's applied to a country intro à la Chet Atkins. Play all of the eighth notes in the first measure with downstrokes, as this will set you up for the upbeats in the second measure. Be sure to play with the tips of your fingers—you really want to be able to hear the E string ring out as you are playing the slides in the first measure.

This next example is reminiscent of the style of Johnny Cash. Shift your hand up a half step from open position—you'll want to play the 2nd and 4th frets with your index and ring fingers, respectively. Try to play a nice, smooth gradual bend throughout all of beat 4. This long gradual bend is a perfect example of the need for multi-finger support of bends.

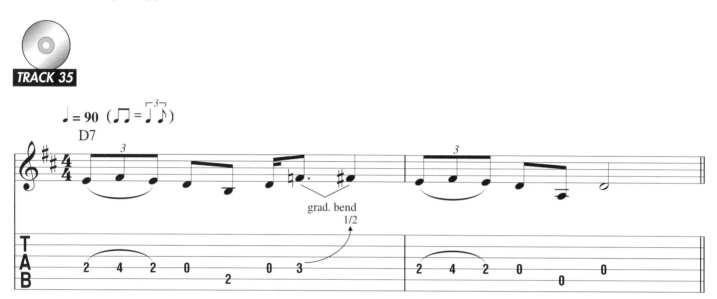

Your index finger plays a significant role in this lick. It will be used for a *fingerroll.* A fingerroll is executed by fretting notes on the same fret of neighboring strings with one finger. This is not to be confused with barring the notes across two adjacent strings; in a roll, each note is played independently. In the second measure, roll your index finger from the E to the B on the A string. This roll will mute the E while you quickly move to the B. In measure 4, be sure to bend the G with your middle finger.

A pull-off from the pinky to the ring finger can be difficult to manage, so take things easy and make sure it's clean. For this example, use alternate picking starting with an upstroke—this will line you up perfectly for the accent on beat 3 as well as the downstroke for the F♯ in the second measure. Also, don't neglect the staccato mark at the end of measure 2, as it will give you time to set up the rake in the last measure. Rakes work really well on guitar, especially when the notes ascend on the downbeat, but in this example we have the opposite scenario—the rake starts on the upbeat and requires an upstroke. An upstroke rake will require you to "flatten out" or angle your pick toward you—with the back of the hand turned up—as you pull across the strings. The opposite is true for executing a downstroke rake, by the way; the back of your hand should be turned away from you. Slanting the pick during a rake will help create a uniform sound.

Here's a combination of downstroke rake and hybrid picking styles. Play the first three 16th notes with a downstroke rake and the last 16th note with your middle finger. This will make that fourth note pop.

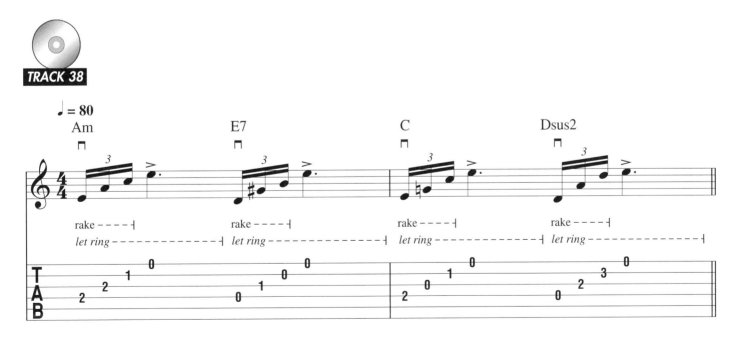

R&B/Funk

In the lick below, resist the urge to play a hammer-on in beat 2 in the second measure. To avoid the hammer-on, play the 1st-fret slide with your middle finger. To ensure a strong attack, play a downstroke for beat 2 as well as the slide. Throughout the lick, keep your fingers spread apart while playing with your pinky and ring fingers—this will help your frethand accuracy.

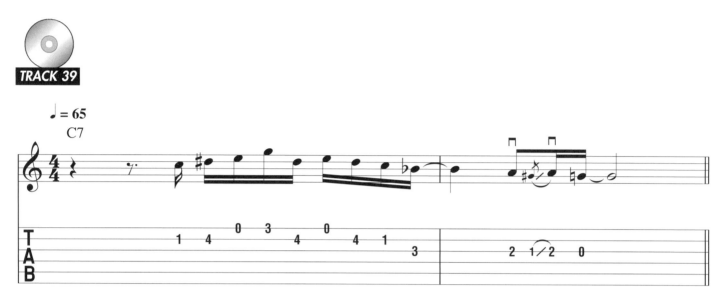

This progression is reminiscent of the "Motown Sound." If you play the first bend with an upstroke, the following open E string can be played accurately with a downstroke.

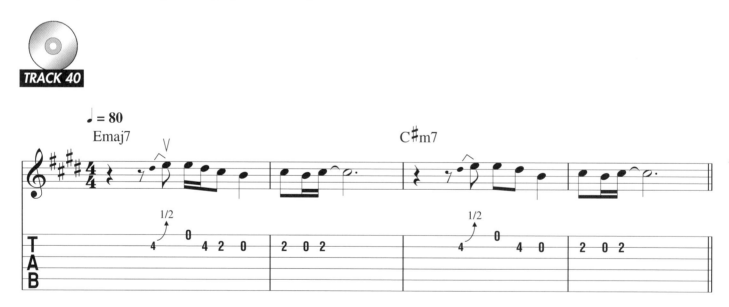

If you are having trouble with the timing in the beginning of this riff, remember that the lick will start right after your foot taps out beat 2. The hammer-ons in the first and second measures will keep your alternate picking consistent and lined up on the beat. Once you've completed the B–C hammer-on in measure 2, be sure to roll your ring finger onto the F. Here again, the roll method will automatically mute the A string and get you right to the next note at the same time.

TRACK 41

This next example has a Tower of Power flavor to it. In order to play the vibrato in the first measure properly, you must use your index finger for the C♯ and your middle finger for the F♯. The vibrato can be easily executed from that position.

TRACK 42

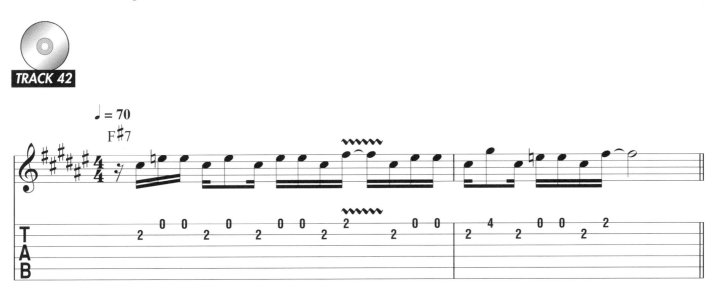

Can you decipher the call-and-response in this next lick? In the second measure, the short eighth note articulation in beat 1 requires you to use your frethand to stop the string. Your middle finger plays an important role here—it's used to create the articulation, execute the finger roll from F♯–A, and mute the E string during the string skip.

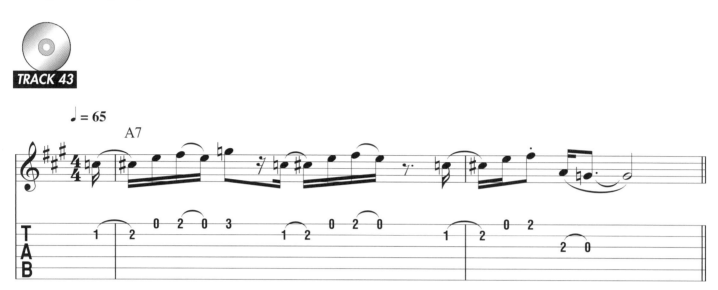

Each phrase below should be started with a downstroke. Your index and ring fingers will suffice for all of the hammer-on/pull-off combinations. A more complex version of this lick would actually involve a C hammer-on with a double pull-off (D–C–B). As you climb the guitar technique ladder, feats like this should become very easy to manage. One way to expedite this process is to attack notes with your frethand (without using your pick).

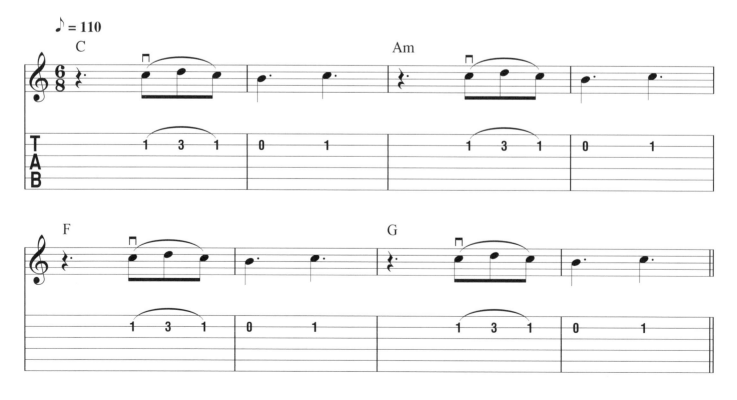

This next example is similar to the previous one, except we're in the key of G major here. Again, the melody is altered to exploit the appropriate chord tones.

TRACK 45

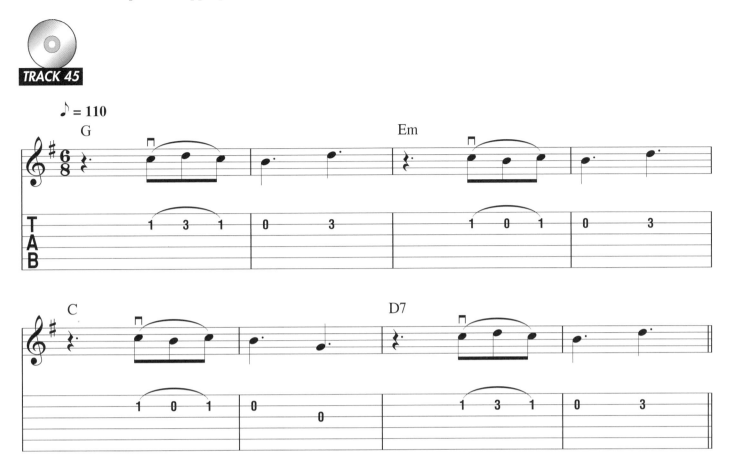

Start this riff with an upstroke and pay attention to the articulation as it reinforces the rhythmic flavor of the phrase. As before, you will need to use your frethand to mute the appropriate strings throughout the phrase. Practice muting the strings with your remaining fingers—i.e., the fingers not fretting any notes. This will come in handy when you need to play the same fret on adjacent strings or when you need to skip a string with a finger roll.

TRACK 46

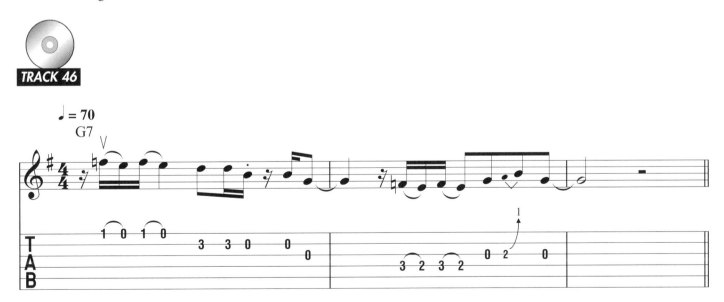

Here we have a simple pull-off to the open B string with mixed groupings of 16th notes. Odd-number groupings can sometimes mess with the picking direction of a phrase. To avoid possible problems, pick the beginning of each grouping with an upstroke. This will allow the anticipated D at the end of the phrase to be attacked strongly. A strong attack is needed for the sustained vibrato.

TRACK 47

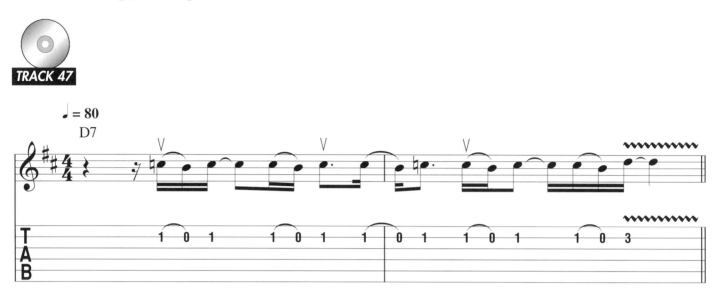

In this example, start the lick with an upstroke. You will then be lined up for a strong downstroke attack on every downbeat.

TRACK 48

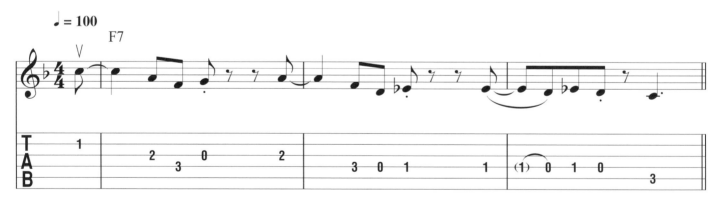

This example utilizes one of the great contemporary musical relationships—the use of the ♭7th and 3rd. The relationship between them is known as a *tritone*, and it helps to create the dominant chord's characteristic sound. A tritone interval is defined as six half steps from one note to the next. You can see it in the first two notes (G–C♯) of the phrase. When playing this example, each grouping should begin with an upstroke. The following pull-offs should give you ample time to wind up for the next upstroke. It is important in the first measure to fret with your fingertips—this can help the notes to ring out for their full values.

TRACK 49

This lick is a variation on the previous example, but here it's over a D7 chord and the tritone has been replaced by a perfect 5th (G–C). This requires you to keep your fingers well spaced and on their tips so the appropriate notes can ring for their full values. The pull-offs are to be played quickly.

TRACK 50

Jazz

Notice how the open G string works over the first two chords. First, try to play the riff with your index and ring fingers on the 2nd and 4th frets. Once you are comfortable with that, go back and play the riff again with your middle finger and pinky on the 2nd and 4th frets. This is good practice in playing in multiple positions.

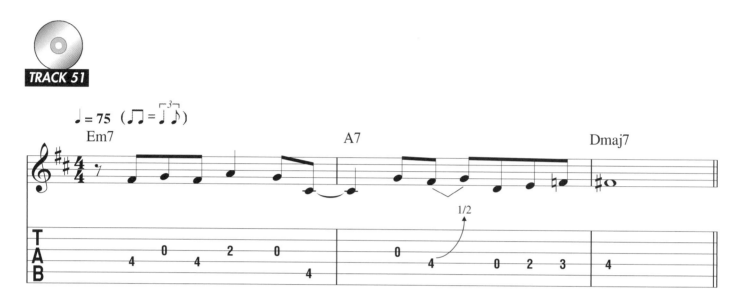

Stick to traditional fingerings here—index finger on the 1st fret, middle finger on the 2nd fret, etc. In measure 2, if you run into trouble with the 16th note triplet, you can place your index and ring fingers at the 2nd and 4th frets, respectively. Again, use alternate picking whenever possible; it's faster, more efficient, and easier to control.

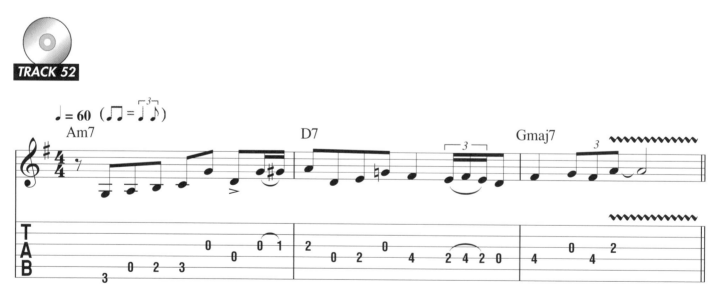

This next swinging little lick includes a slight reference to Bach's *Two-Part Inventions.*

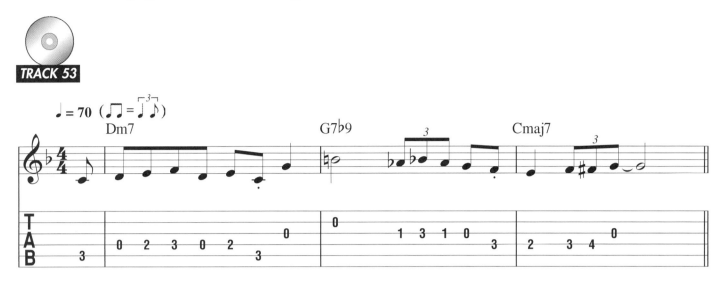

Here's a ii–V–I chord progression in E♭ major so you can see how the open G string works over chords that aren't in open position. Hold the notes with longer durations (C♭ and A♭) for their full values.

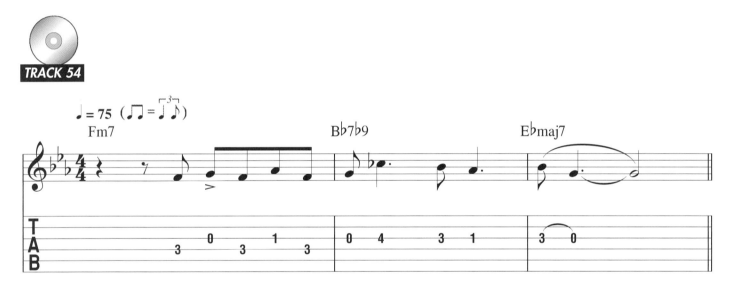

Here's a more challenging lick over an Am7 chord. Use alternate picking, and stick to traditional fingering—you'll thank me when you get to the double stops! Fret with your fingertips so the open string can ring through the double stops.

The most important part of this next example is the quick tempo. Work on this one slowly at first. Once you get it, try this clever trick: When playing at fast tempos in 4/4, shift your counting from every beat to every *other* beat (i.e., instead of counting 1–2–3–4, count 1–2, with the "new" 2 being the "old" 3). Basically, feel the song as if it were in half time—counting in groups of two half notes instead of groups of four quarter notes. At a fast tempo, this can be much easier for your brain to process, and you'll get to the true flavor of the phrase.

You will need to mute the notes marked P.M.—for *palm mute*—with your pickhand. Notice how the phrase C♯–C–B repeats itself while each time ending on a different string. In the third measure, there is even a string skip. I know what you are thinking, "Kyle, I keep hitting the other string as I try to skip!" Fear not! You can either mute the strings with your pickhand—which is essentially continuing to palm-mute the strings—or with the 1st finger of your frethand until you attack the F♯. The latter method is a little more tricky. Try each method and see which works best for you.

TRACK 56

This line contains a number of idiosyncratic jazz-style passing tones. As far as the chord progression is concerned, I find it very helpful to use just one chord throughout a song or section to really explore all of the possibilities of a tonality—it's almost like a "snapshot" of all the sounds that are available for a chord. Once you are comfortable with a tonality, you can then re-apply it to a chord progression—and as a result, it will be easier for you to create coherent solos.

Here's a great exercise to improve your vibrato technique. Play a note and increase the vibrato speed from quarter notes to eighth notes, to eighth note triplets, and finally to 16th notes. This will improve your control and expression on the guitar. Joe Pass, Jim Hall, and Pat Metheny all have precise control over their vibrato.

TRACK 57

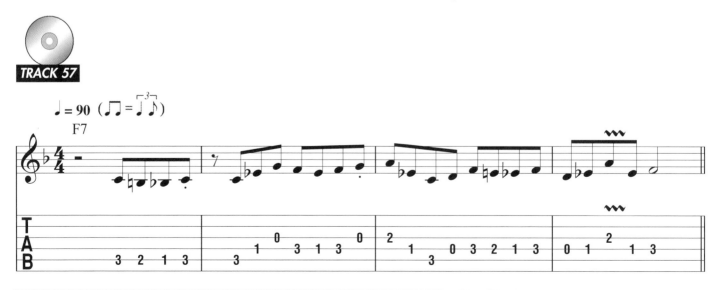

This example is based on the classic "rhythm changes"—the I–VI–ii–V chord progression that is an essential part of the jazz idiom. This example is in the key of C major, so the progression is C–A7–Dm–G7. The lick starts on the downbeat of beat 2, so be sure to start the phrase with a downstroke. Practice the line slowly at first and gradually work the tempo up to around 120 b.p.m. A healthy handful of jazz musicians play this progression at a fast tempo. Notice the placement of the open B and E notes on the upbeats of the phrase—this helps to propel the groove. When you play two consecutive open strings, it's important that you palm-mute the first string as you attack the next open string. It's always good to experiment with different hand positions for muting. For instance, if you are about to play an upstroke, try using the base of your thumb—a slight variation of a palm-mute—to stifle the open string.

TRACK 58

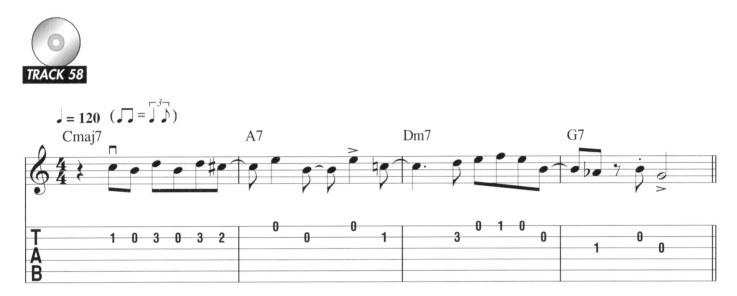

This lick is also played over rhythm changes, but this time we're in G major, so the progression is G–E7–Am–D7. Now, class, can you tell me anything that stands out to you? If you answered that it's the same riff with a couple of different notes in it, you would be correct. The open E and B notes are still harmonically relevant to the chords. Make sure that the *anticipated* notes (notes that come just before the downbeat) are played as upstrokes; this will help you to keep track of the beat with your right hand. Also, follow the same palm-muting instructions as in the last example for the open B and E strings.

TRACK 59

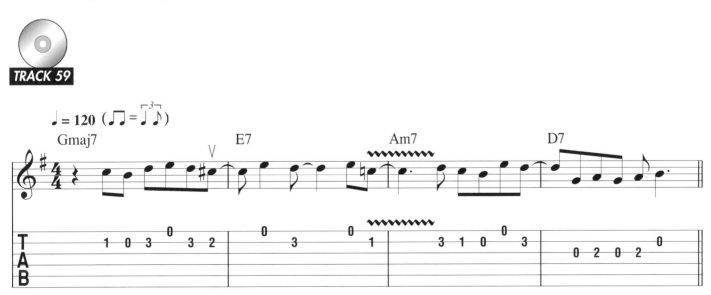

Here's one more lick over rhythm changes, but with a few variations. This time, the progression is not only repeated, but the second tonic chord (F) is substituted by a dominant chord (A7) in the third measure, so the progression is Fmaj7–D7–Gm7–C7–A7–D7–Gm7–C7–Fmaj7. This lick is good practice in playing cross-string phrases, and it can really help you to hear the alternate A7 harmony in measure 3.

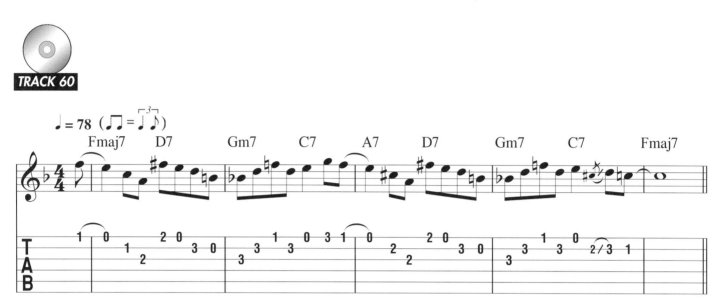

This lick makes use of a drone note—in this case, an open D string. If you have trouble picking across those two strings in the first measure, try incorporating the hybrid picking technique. Use your pick for the open D string, and then pluck the B and G strings with your remaining fingers. This approach is great for when you have to play notes that are two or more strings apart. Make sure to control the durations of the open strings with your frethand. Most of the time you'll be able to mute the string with your index finger.

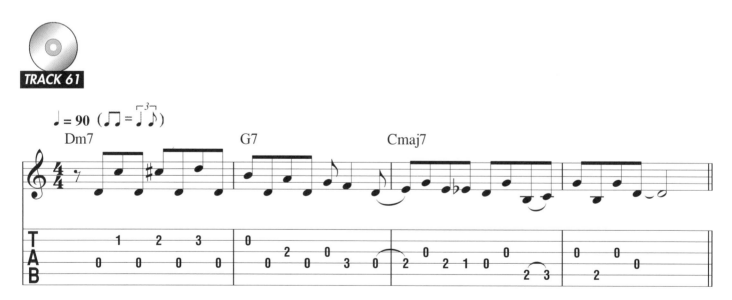

Bluegrass

You may notice that a number of these mostly slow bluegrass examples are in the key of G major. This is because the banjo—a key component of bluegrass music—is tuned in G major. This also means that the relative E minor key is also applicable.

For this first example, keep your fingers posed right above each fret. This will aid you in making a quick return to the B string. In the second measure, the slide is best executed with your ring finger, as this will set you up for the pull-off (F#–E) with your middle finger.

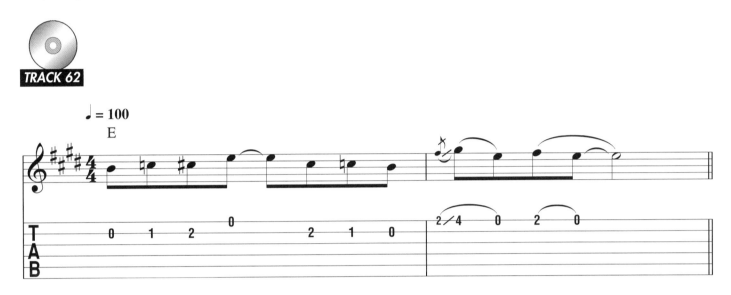

Resist the urge to let the open strings in the first measure ring sympathetically; you will need to use your pick-hand to mute the strings. In the second measure, set up your frethand fingers as if you were going to play an open Am chord. Now, you can simply pick up your fingers to play the open strings of the phrase. In the third measure, play the slide with your middle finger.

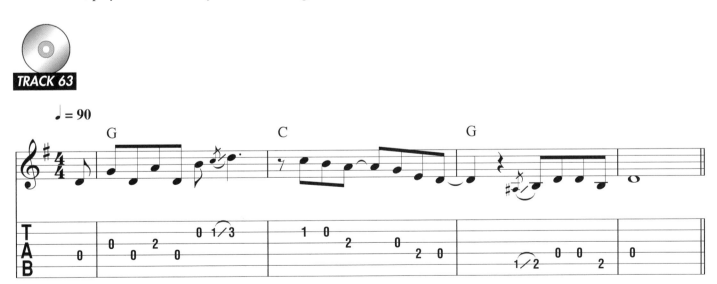

In the first measure, use your pinky to slide into the G. The following F♯–E pull-off can then be played easily with your ring finger as you descend through the rest of the lick.

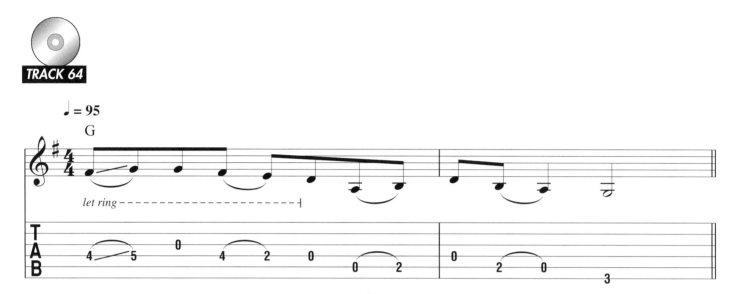

In this next lick, the chords are best stopped with the index, middle, and ring fingers of your frethand. Simply rest your index and middle fingers across the open strings as you are about to play the B♭ with your ring finger. Also, note that the hammer-ons in this example use a mix of both eighth note and dotted eighth note rhythmic patterns.

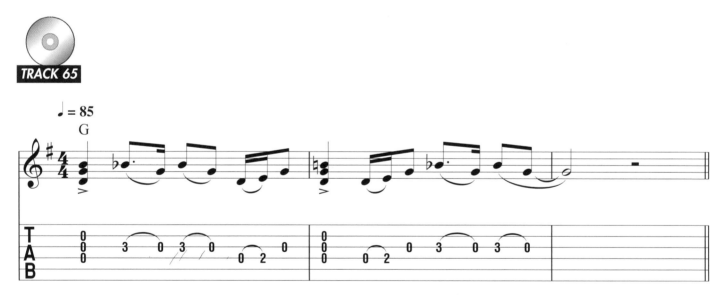

You will need to let the E string ring on in this example, so be sure to play with your frethand fingertips. In the third measure, you'll need to resist the urge to play a double pull-off to the open G string—the open G must also be attacked. That open G will give you a little extra time to reach for the F♯; if you have trouble reaching that F♯ with your pinky, try re-positioning your frethand thumb. You may be able to gain some extra reach by moving your thumb parallel to the neck.

The second measure of this example offers a mixture of cross-string and adjacent string notes. Try both the hybrid and traditional picking approaches to see which one works best for you. Holding your frethand fingers in the shape of a C chord will also help you to play this measure. Be aware that all of the notes are meant to ring throughout the measure. In the third measure, keep your index finger barred at the 1st fret so that you can easily play both the hammer-on and pull-off. The bend should be played with your ring finger.

Employ alternate picking to ensure the proper inflection of the phrase, especially on the repeated D in the first measure. In the second measure, play the slide with your middle finger. This will make it easy to play the D and the decending slide.

TRACK 68

Notice how the 16th note hammer-ons aid in maintaining the alternate-picking pattern. Start the lick with an upstroke, and you will be in good shape for the rest of the line.

TRACK 69

Practice this example slowly and gradually work it up to speed. The hammer-on in the second measure needs to be played with an upstroke—this will help to set up the string jump in the third measure. Remain in open position for the last two measures of the riff.

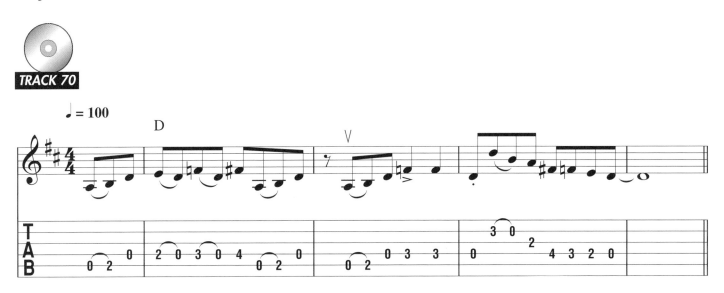

In this example, try both the traditional and hybrid picking methods. Being able to do both will prepare you for a multitude of applications. The traditional alternating pick method can help you with string jumps, while the hybrid method can give you a mixed sound texture—forceful downbeats and lighter upbeats.

In the first measure, play the slide with your middle finger and the D with your index finger. The open B string in the next measure will give you enough time to get back into open position.

This line sounds more like a banjo the faster you play it. Starting the line with a downstroke will set you up for all of the hammer-ons and cross-string jumps in this lick. In the second measure, you'll need to play the double stop slide quickly.

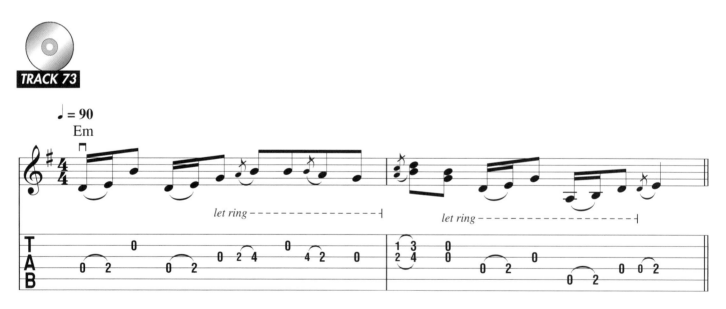

This next example is based on groups of three 16th notes. Play the first measure as all downstrokes, as this will ensure an even sound on the double stops. Use your middle finger to play the D and your index and ring fingers for F# and G double stops. This will put you in position for the rest of the lick.

TRACK 74

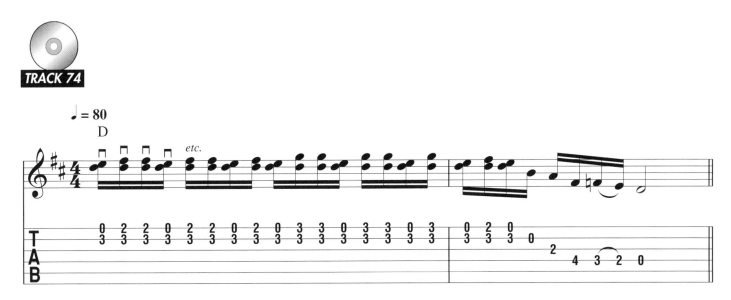

Here's another riff that is based on a grouping of three 16th notes. Make sure you fret with your fingertips so the open E string isn't muted. Play the first pull-off in the first measure with an upstroke—this will line you up for the cross-string jump in the second measure.

TRACK 75

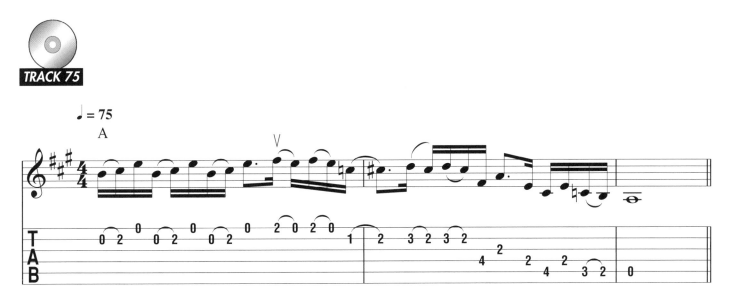

The tempo of this last example makes the use of the open strings that much more significant. If you keep your hand in the shape of an open Am or C chord, you'll stand a better chance of cleanly executing this lick at a fast tempo.

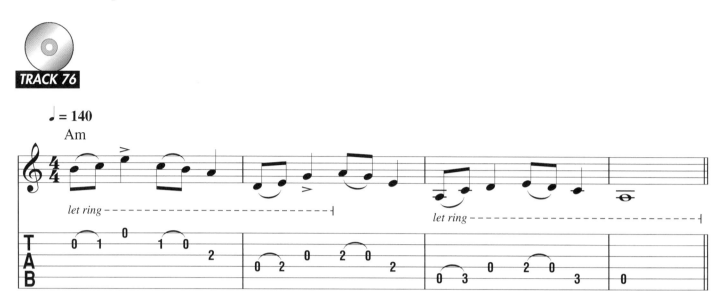

Afterword

The more knowledge one gains in the study of music, the more one can appreciate the different styles of music for their simplicity, complexity, or lyricism. Learning different styles like rock, blues, jazz, and bluegrass isn't necessarily about being better or more expressive—it's about each style having its own inflections and vocabulary, and getting all of that into your head and fingers so you can develop your own style. Always keep an open mind, and try to learn from a variety of music and cultures. It will make your own music and life richer.